LANGUISH
Love And Other Lies

Languish:
Love and Other Lies

Alex MacPherson

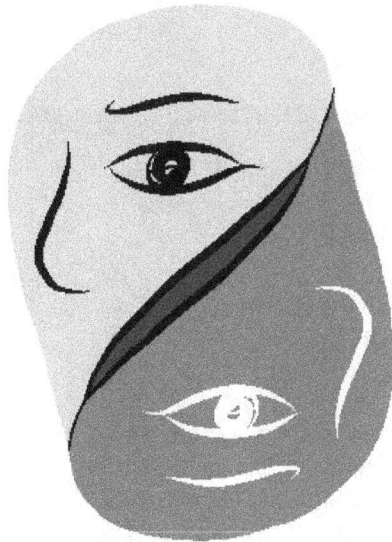

Mythical Echo Publishing
2019

First Printing: 2019

ISBN-13: 978-1-7332686-0-8 (Paperback)

ISBN-13: 978-1-7332686-1-5 (Ebook)

Ordering Information:

Mythical Echo Publishing
Portland, OR 97201
MythicalEchoPublishing@gmail.com

Special discounts are available on quantity purchases by corporations, associations, educators, and others. For details, contact the publisher at the above listed email address or author's website below.

www.mythicalechopublishing.com

Dedication

To Pierre, the one being in my life that keeps me going, no matter the wacky situations life brings.

May you always have enough gooshy food and sunbeams.

Contents

I - Love

Photosynthesis

I can't tell you that I care
It comes off weird when I say it aloud
  You are much like the sun
  A star in its own right
But also important to those near
  A purveyor of life
  A collector of love
And I am merely one of many
  Who craves the sunlight
  Yet fear being scorched
Though I would drown in Calamine seas
  If given the opportunity

I would write you a hundred operas
  Performed by the greatest of all time
  In languages around the world
So people would understand your glory
I would paint a thousand portraits
  In every style of art known
  Making up new ones along the way
For the world to gaze upon you
  And feel an iota of the warmth I get
  From seeing your smile

I would find a way to match
  The floral-powder tinge of sweet that you
emanate
  And the world could be drunk on your
smell

3

But it would all be vague forgery
  To just being in the same room
  As an earthbound goddess
I cannot tell you these things
  The fear of exile is worse than any death
  Leaving only admiration from the shadows
Warm contemplation
  An unfilled craving for blisters

Burn

I was lost in your eyes
  Drowning in a color I
  Didn't know existed
My breath stolen
  By lips as soft
  As the petals
Of the most exotic flowers
  Enraptured by each word
  As though they were secrets
And not grocery lists
  My heart thundering
  Harder and faster
The closer you are
  Each touch a spark
  Fire from your fingertips
I long to burn again

Electric

I never know
What to expect
Underneath my fingertips
As I touch your skin
Either the softest silk
An electric charge
Or some beautiful combination
Leaving my hands
Wanting nothing more
Than to stay
In your embrace

The Slave

He gives himself completely
Wanting to be loved
  Hated
    Excited
    Humiliated
He kneels at my feet
  Content as my footstool
    Even as muscles fatigue
    And exhaustion sets in

All the while
  Giving me ideas
    Of humiliations to come
      Relationships to destroy

He confesses details
  As easily as he confesses desire
    Wanting the disgrace
    Wanting the shame
He shares how to hurt him
  In every life aspect
    With every old lover
    And secret yearning
I debase him to the world
  Abolishing his past
    Twisting his existence
    Into my desire
Yet I do these things

Punish his wrongs
Twist his behaviors
Knowing full well
These are his true wishes
That I merely play out for him
Like a puppet
I have my place
I am the Master, and yet I am the Slave

Name

Your name is as beautiful
As watching the sunset
Over the Atlantic
In a small Irish town
I can taste it
In every raindrop of the morning
It sits heavy on my lips
As I fall asleep at night
And lingers on every breath I take in

9

Strings

Each sound you draw with your fingertips
 Finds its way inside my soul
In a single moment
 I am completely transfixed
Nothing exists beyond this symphony

Trouble

I should have known
  You'd be trouble
    With 6 capital Ts
I don't care how stutter inducing that
        may sound
  It would have given me pause
    To have known that before
I'd like to think
  But of course
    I'd still do it all again
Probably in the exact same way

Foolish Love

Date that idiot
  No, the other one
    That girl who makes you swoon
As she steals your cat in the night
The one who likes guitars
  And makes you question yourself
    Like you never knew how to love before
Because no one else made it feel
  As though being punched in the stomach
    By monsterous butterflies
Was something you craved

II - Longing

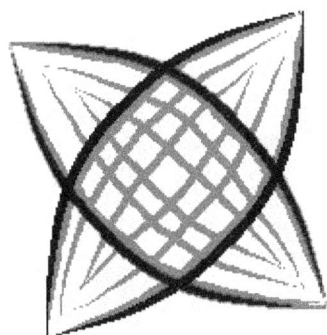

Awakening

Every time you touch me
　Each caress of my skin
　　I lose myself in you
My thoughts dissipate
　Into ether clouds
　　And all I know that's real
Is the feeling of your hand
　Awakening my flesh
　　As though I had never been
Never lived
　Prior to this moment

　All else stripped away
Your hand may hold mine
　But your touch
　　Reaches farther than bone
Piercing my soul
　Waking me
　　Showing me life

And I can never thank you
　Even if you stop touching my skin
　　Pull your hands back
Retreat to safety
　I am forever changed
　　Forever craving
The next embrace

Starving for your touch
Just to feel again
Something lost for so long
All illusions fade
Yet this remains
Shaping me
With a single impression

Twenty Feet

You're 20 feet away
But it may as well be
The Earth to the Sun
   If my arms have to feel this empty
Eight minutes at the speed of light
Could never be fast enough
   To get me back in your arms
And 20 feet now
May as well take a lifetime
   If it's not hand in hand with you

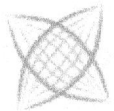

Touch

Feeling your lips caress mine
  Your soft skin against my palms
    The gentle gasp as I pull you closer
Straining your belt loops
  I want you closer to me
    Always closer
I want to breathe you in

The Zone

I am not in the Girlfriend Zone
That is not how I am seen
  I am not worthy of time
  When the sun is shining

I am only allowed over
When darkness shrouds my appearance
  No roommates could pick me out
  From a crowd of random nobodies

You don't use the word fetish
But I am not a desired asset
  At least not to the public
  Where my existence is clandestine

Being with me brings up shadows
Too dark to face in day
  People might know
  They may suspect
They might consider me human
And not merely a commodity

I am not given choices
Any sliver of attention
  Must be repaid with interest
  Scraps of connection
Fuel my existence

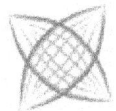

For I subsist only in the Fuck Zone
You have put me here
  No thought to any possibility
  That I would have emotions
Or persist outside your desires

I'm only here for your urges
To fulfill what you need
  And to leave when you're done with me
  No need to say goodbye
I know where all the exits are
And how to stay quiet

Of course they'll never know
  I am very good at my role
It's all I'm permitted to do

Ashes

"How are you?"
You casually ask
   As though my life wasn't for your
consumption
   Putting you before everything else
   Destroying myself in the process
Not that it matters

I'm not her

I'm the one who gets you bail
   She's the one who gets goodnight
messages
No matter where you are
   Or who your body embraces
I make sure you live to the weekend
She's the one you spend it with
   Shelving the world away
   And anyone else inside it

   I'm the one with the scars of pieces
removed
Etched waterfalls of tears
 A cold hearth remaining

I gave it all freely
But the pain is still the same
   As if it were stolen by moonlight arsonists
Every tear stained shirt

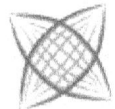

Every silent car ride
A reminder of who I fail to be
Perhaps next year it won't matter
    Like scores of people before you
Tossing me to the wind
    As you do to the ashes of something long
gone
One day you may have a flash
    A memory of light and heat
    Still unaware of how fire works
    Consuming the subject
    Forgetting the source material
A tree cannot be burned twice
    Without stopping to regrow

I hope she figures out a way
    To cease self immolation
The forest is weary of your offerings

Sharp

You are
  Much too sharp
I am
  Not sharp enough
My teeth
  Are too soft
    To rip off this flesh

My nails
  Always break
    Before I can penetrate skin
I have
  No way
    To let out the sharpness inside

The only angles
  Come from shoulder blades
And how far out
  My hip bones can protrude

Maybe she'll love me now
  When my cheekbones are taut
    Like a piano wire

The garrote of my ribs
  Each holding cloth
    As close as I hold self contempt

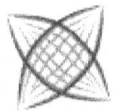

Countable vertabral mountains
  One for every spoken slight
Each dip for a silence
  Broken only through screams

Every measured meal
  Another bar in this prison window
    That only looks toward a wall
      Should I get any ideas

They always say
  I look like she did growing up
This living skeleton
  Did not choose their lineage
And is unscrewing the bars
  Slowly
Each angle ever sharper
  Every breath a bit more shallow

I wonder if they'll say
  I still look like her
    Lying In the ground

III - Loss

Fire

Being with you
  Was like trying to stand next to fire
Raging around me
    Consuming my world
Until all I knew was embers
  And I had to rebuild with ash
In a spot now so cold
    It feels like nothing will grow here again
I stand alone
  Shivering

Muse

You might have been the muse
  For endless words
    Whose beauty pales
  By sheer comparison
But you were also the muse
  For destructive metaphors
    And complex agony
  Aching from within

Removing the words from inside
  Takes away that agony
    Along with that beauty
  Leaving a blank slate
To start anew
  And free myself

Communication

I like it when you break my heart
  The familiar cadence of your rejection
It reminds me of home

Your sigh is like the starting bell
  A signal to take my corner
My defense is always silence
To avoid further screams into the night
  Like banshees during a plague

You don't actually hear my shrieks
  I'm much too polite for that
Even humor was a failed attempt
Communication left rusting
  Leaving only one available channel
The volume knob won't move
All I hear is static
  And the remnants of repeated stale
sermons

We only talk in the round
  Remove the sharp things
Cover all the corners
Take out every implement of destruction
  Except your biting words
All but searing the flesh
An acrid tongue sharing twisted thoughts
  Scars unseen by the many
Sterilize the area

Nothing enters that can cause harm
Enough infection already exists
Permeating synapses
  Tainting every thought and word
Only viewable beyond the moment
To everyone
  Except my own mangled perception

The preachers change
The sermon stays the same
  Perhaps I need a new religion
Though the cost is less for appliances

Syllable

I knew exactly what you were going to
say
  Before it even left your lips
   I should have been prepared
    From the first syllable you spoke
For each one to be your last
  To me

But I never listen to that voice
  The one in my head that suggests danger
   It speaks too softly for me to hear
    As I was busy listening to the sound
Of my heart breaking at your every word

Capturing Smoke

I'm not the last person you talk to at night
  Or the first one in the morning
    Even when I'm the one in your bed
I'll never be able to say
  What everyone else can
    Or tell stories
Nearly as interesting

I guess that's my fault
  For being a bore
    Or living a real life
Where shit just happens
  And we deal
    I'll never be the fantasy
Or even just enough
  To truly hold your interests
    It would be like capturing smoke
And all I have
  Is a mousetrap

Stoking the Fires

Congratulations!
I didn't think we would reach this point
  where I have officially given up
  I am done fighting you
I am done trying to understand the constant
paranoid enigmas
  Pouring out of your mind
  Like a faucet welded to never turn off

It takes so much effort
  Beyond anything Sisyphus could imagine
  In his wildest Salvia nightmares
To merely understand how awful I must be
in your mind
  Feeling the omnipresent torture of my
mere existence

You can say whatever you want about me
  I do implore you however
  Please regale me with these legends of
my horrors
As I must have ingested some amnesiac
And fail to recollect my time working for the
Spanish Inquisition

You have ripped out every strand
connecting yourself to me
  Before any roots could possibly lay hold
  I cannot continue to chase at the frayed
edges

Attempting to stay warm from a quilt made
of
  Dismembered emotions
  And lies brought forth from unseen
demons

I would rather freeze alone
  Than try to stay warm in your fires
  Constantly stoked with pieces of my being
I cannot continue down this labyrinthian trail
  I have already lost so much of myself
  This consumption will be my ending

IV - Lies

Normal

I've been held by depression
  More than by any lover
    More than by my mother
  Who never thought I had a problem

Depression isn't real
  And medication is just a crutch
    Your sadness will pass
  Just disappear
The way your friends all have
  And you'll be back to normal

  Where normal is knowing
Exactly how tall that bridge is
  How it feels to never hear silence
    And the difference between sharp and
dull
  Ripping through flesh that never saw it
coming

Pretending that every undertaking
  Is worth getting up from staring at the
ceiling all night
    Only passing out briefly when your body
can't stand to be awake any longer
  Never knowing which dreams are coming
this time

Normal is constant questions
  Ever on the edge of self destruction

Is this pain from cancer or stress?
How long can I pretend I'm ok?
Mirrors show my dark circles
But I'm fine
Fine

I'm great, please tell me about your crisis
If nothing else, I listen well
This town is full of actors
Keeping each other as far away as
possible
From knowing anything real about
somebody else
I know my role
This is the normal
Almost comforted by the emptiness
This tea is as dark as the circles
But it's fine
Fine

Wrong

You told me one day I'd hate you
I told you that was a lie
One of us was wrong

Sigh

Beautiful words
  Spoken under the covers

Never hold true
  In the light of day

Bad Guy

I am the Bad Guy
Always the villain
Never the logical one
With the plan
The one who takes charge
Just the Bad Guy

What was today's reason?
How did I cause a failure now?
Because I can't read minds?
Or I did something in a different way than
you wanted?
Maybe I just said a word
In a tone exactly like some other person
Who also failed the tests

Maybe I didn't ask you something
Which is clearly part of my evil plan
Not bothering to mention
The last time you asked how I was
Involved me losing blood and
consciousness
And even then
Only because
It was literally
In your stumbling path

Did you know

41

Other people have issues too?
I know
 I speak the crazy
  That implies others have meaning in their
lives
  Something else to take up time
Clearly bookmarked in your head

  The calendar shows nine days
  Since the last 4 am screaming
All my faults and wrongs
  Scattered to the wind
   Eggshells would be a reprieve
  To walking on these sharpened lego
pieces

  Every day a new layout
  Yesterday's mines are reset
New ones strategically placed
  Some days bring peace
   Others involve removing shrapnel
  Never quite getting out the slivers
I will die of metal poisoning
  Before I let you see me bleed

Takeover

The shadow takes over
  When I cannot move
    It breathes for the body
  Forcing lungs to squeeze air
Like water from a sponge

It sounds more like me every day
  As I slither in emptiness
    Allowing the takeover
      Not sure who I see in the mirror
      The cracks in my skin seem darker
  The inverse of glitter

Good question, Trent
  "What have I become?"
    A tired reprieve
  Escalating to a lifelong siesta
An existence of pure apathy

Apologies

I am sorry for never doing anything right
For repeatedly picking the wrong path in life
   For making decisions that are constant
disappointments
I apologize for choosing my own happiness
  After years of squandering it
   And putting other people first

   Please forgive me for never listening
  Or doing things unlike how you fervently
told me to do them
   For doing anything that wasn't run past
you first
  I implore you
I have clearly chosen incorrectly
   I have been wrong
   I am always wrong
  And I do nothing but destroy people's lives
I have failed you
   I have failed everyone

  So I apologize
I am sorry to anyone who hears these
words
   And assumes for a single minute
That they are anything but drenched
  In sarcasm and vile platitudes
I am done being sorry

44

V - Languish

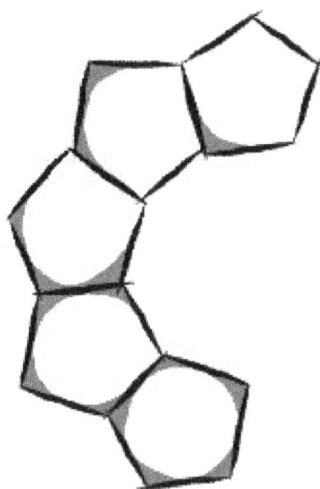

3am

It's 3 in the morning by the time I get out of
bed
My day has already come and gone
But now I'm finally not asleep
I bring myself to shower for the first time in
six days
No one else has been aware of it
Until now

This land between anxiety and depression
is slowly killing me
Some days I feel stuck
Like invisible hands hold me to a bed
That is no longer comfortable
Yet still better than standing
Some days I actually have the energy to do
100 things
None of which are what needs to be
done

There are scratches on my skin from
trying to remove dirt with nails instead of
sponges
When I finally do laundry
It still never feels clean
Every shower is like a torture and release
at the same time

I do an incredible impression of a
functional human

47

But the act has been slipping of late
I no longer know who sees the mask
  And who has seen this wretched creature
underneath

The worst part is that I'm starting not to care
  This is my best impersonation of a useful
person
I've seen better acting in middle school
plays
Yet I cannot take the bow and finally rest
I spin like a dervish
  Dizzy from the whirl
  Dizzy from the world
It all travels past so quickly

I start to forget the little things
  Did I go to work this week?
    I can't remember the last time I checked
the mail
  I'm pretty sure I had a conscious moment
this month
Where I wasn't shrouded by a blanket of
  Dissociation
  Exhaustion
  And whelm

She can yell for days
But no one is more angry at me
  Than me
  Maybe tomorrow I will get up at a normal
time

Grab coffee like a human and plod away
As though I were a responsible adult
　Maybe tomorrow, I say
One more snooze on the alarm can't hurt
One more
　Maybe the next tomorrow instead

My head is full of bees today
I can only move to feed the cat
　Lest he eats my face
Focusing on retaining my cartilage
　Floof is content
I remain nauseous
　Is it still seasickness if you've never been
on a boat
Can you get jet lag from cruise ships

Who decided this system
　Where I suddenly must decide
　　Between living
　And truly being alive

Scars

People rarely inquire where the scars
come from
And when they do
They don't expect the truth
Angry kitten
Vengeful garbage disposal
Crime fighting accident
Hilarity ensues from the story
They can't stand to hear
Extreme isolation
I can't get out of bed
Or maybe
I just need to feel something
Like I'm actually attached to this body
Even as it kills me
I'm more than just a pilot in this meat robot
Some people think of me as human
But I'm moreso an inept foreman
My body a construction zone
It has been zero days without an accident

Silence

The silence
  Is harder than
    Any vile word you could spit
At least then I could know my position
  We call it silence but it's merely the
absence of talking
    Everything else becomes so loud
  The heater in my wall becomes a startling
creature screaming in the night
To remind me that the only one keeping me
warm right now is myself
  Rainfall on the roof sounds more like
shrapnel
    Waiting to dig into my flesh
Should I go outside
  The worst, of course
    Is the ever-present low thudding of my
own palpitations
  Hearing the emptiness of heartbeats
No longer echoed in return
    What I would not give for real silence

Forcing the Smile

I'm not okay
  The scab on my wrist is indicative of that
But I go on
  Forcing the smile
    Pretending I'm fine
  Whole, while waiting
    To do it again
  Maybe better this time
No really, I'm fine
  Just do what you will
I've got time
  So they say
    I checked out days ago
  I don't feel time passing
    I don't feel anything
  Even the rain on my head
Walking in the bitter cold
  The feeling doesn't creep in
    You can't hurt something that's already
dead

Flint

Without looking
  Tell me
    What color are my eyes?
      Which side has the dimple?
        How do I like my coffee?
Or maybe
  Something simple
    How many tears have already fallen
down my cheek today?
      How many times have I silently left as
you screamed into the void?
      How many ways can you destroy
someone, without even a glance?

You don't need to look at me anymore
  You already know how well you can maim
    Ripping thru emotions
    Like wolves do flesh
      To remove whatever independence I
have left

I look away from the rage in your eyes
  Which you claim is never there
    But I see nothing else
      The angry way you wipe a counter
      That was never clean enough

Hurdling past me to find a missing vice
  Stopping at nothing to adhere blame

With minions agreeing as they nip at your heels

You've never met someone like me
  So these tactics are merely show dressing
    I did not get the script ahead of time
I'm not one for playing my part

  Scream all you like
  Break every dish
  Threaten every vicious cruelty
I smile inside while you berate me
  I give no weight to your destruction
    The tornado is nothing but kite fodder

I have done this dance before
  Time and time again
    Partners and friends
    Lovers and family
And every time I come out even stronger
  Wiping off the initial shock
    On my scotch guarded heart

We will use paper plates as needed
  Fill my ears with cotton balls
    And know just one thing that you do not

  I'm far more patient than you know
  I have skills you've never seen
You may rage at an unworking appliance
  And attempt to make me feel small
    Until one day you'll have to turn against
the minions   54

As there will be nothing but emptiness
Where I once stood
And fires you could never imagine
Stoked by the flint of my heels
Taking a final walk on the gasoline spray
of your existence

Acknowledgements

I would like to thank all the people who had to read every incarnation and help provide better words and gooder phrases. Or the people who just responded with "oof" when I would text them the next thing that came to me at 3 in the morning. Insomnia sucks, but it's great for weird ideas.

Thank yous specifically go out to several important people, some of whom may like to see their name in text.

Scotty: you've been there for me for years, swapping poems and philosophies, and always having my back. And I thoroughly support you wanting to make youtuber.com for people who mis-type and will end up only watching videos of yams.

Talia: my fucking *Ride or Die*. Even though you moved a million miles away, you've always been there for me. I can't wait to see the next writings your brain comes up with.

Cricket: my tiny bun, my hugger of cats. You're wonderful and I will always support you while change the world for the better. You can do anything you put your mind to, either real career, rock star musician, or just fiddling with something that turns into a cool hobby. You amaze me.

Abby: you are my rock. I know you're surrounded by writers, so the last thing you want is more to read. You've been amazing in times I never thought I would make it, making me feel like I always have a family. I'm so looking forward to John's book, seeing Freyja grow up, all the wacky things that happen in our lives, and knowing we'll always be there for each other.

Thank you to the people who helped with edits and generally going "Ooh" when I said I was writing a poem book. I appreciate it.

And lastly, to the muses. Some know who they are, some never will. Some have been drama, and some will be tapped once more in the future. Some deserve thanks, and some will never be spoken of again. Some made words flow from me faster than I could collect them, and some will always make me unable to talk to them directly. We'll see what the future brings.

About the Author

Alex MacPherson has been writing for what feels like an eternity. Poems, short stories, long stories, books, plays, movies. She loves horror and detective genres, weird science and medical stuff, roller derby, and cats. She also does oil painting,

More importantly, this is Pierre. And he's amazing. The best Emotional Service Animal in the land, he came from Cat Jail (the Humane Society) as a 12 year old guy who just wanted to spend 20 hours a day asleep, often on the author's head.

Portraits of the Pierre doing his best to assist the author. 2018

Pierre says to visit your local shelter and find a buddy.